Echoes of Dreams

Echoes of Dreams

A JOURNEY FROM AFRICA

Anurag Anurag

Anurag Anurag

Contents

1

∽

Vibrant Roots

The Ofori family lived in Ghana, a small West African country situated on the Gulf of Guinea. Ghana is just one of many countries that make up the vast and diverse continent of Africa. Africa is home to over 1.2 billion people, spread across 54 countries. Each country has its unique culture, traditions, and history, but they are all united by a shared sense of identity and pride.

Despite its many challenges, Africa is a land of incredible natural beauty. The continent boasts magnificent landscapes ranging from vast deserts to lush rainforests, and from stunning coastlines to majestic mountains. The wildlife is equally diverse, with species ranging from the mighty African elephant to the elusive leopard.

Africa is also rich in natural resources, including oil, gas, minerals, and agricultural land. These resources have fueled economic growth in many African countries, but they have also been the source of conflict and instability.

Despite these challenges, there is a growing sense of optimism on the continent. More and more countries are working towards economic growth and development, and as African people continue to celebrate their culture and heritage, there is a renewed sense of pride and unity.

The Ofori family is just one example of the rich cultural tapestry that exists across Africa. Despite the economic constraints that limited their opportunities, they remained proud of their heritage and found new and creative ways to celebrate their traditions. Their story is one of resilience, strength, and hope, and it is a testament to the enduring spirit of the African people.

The history of Africa is long and complex. The continent is widely regarded as the cradle of humanity, and it has been home to some of the world's most ancient civilizations. These civilizations left behind a rich legacy of art, architecture, and literature, which continues to inspire people today. However, Africa's history has also been marked by colonization, slavery, and exploitation. These dark chapters of history have left lasting scars on the continent, and they continue to shape the political and economic landscape of many African countries.

Despite these challenges, Africa has made significant strides in recent years. Across the continent, there are examples of innovative solutions to complex problems. African entrepreneurs are starting businesses that are transforming their communities, while African scientists are making breakthroughs in fields like medicine and renewable energy.

As Africa continues to grow and evolve, it is important to remember the incredible diversity that exists across the continent. Each country has its unique strengths and challenges, and each is working towards a brighter future.

The Ofori family's story is just one small part of this larger tapestry. Their experiences are a reminder of the rich cultural heritage that exists across Africa, and of the enduring spirit of the African people. As we look towards the future, let us draw inspiration from their example, and work towards a brighter and more prosperous Africa for all.

2

∽

Aspirations and Boundaries

The decision to migrate was a poignant one for the family. Their homeland had been their home for generations, and the thought of leaving behind their cultural ties was heart-wrenching. However, they were hopeful about what the future held. They dreamed of a better life, one that would allow them to explore new opportunities and experiences.

Samuel, the patriarch of the family, was a historian. He had spent many years studying the history of the region, and he knew that the decision to migrate was not a new one. He shared stories of other families who had made similar journeys, and he reminded his family that they were not alone.

Abena, Samuel's wife, was a calming presence during family discussions. She reassured her children that their cultural heritage would not be lost, even if they were living in a new land. She reminded them that they could still celebrate their traditions and values while also exploring new ones.

Each family member had their own unique aspirations. Kwame, the eldest son, was determined to pursue advanced scientific education. He dreamed of becoming a doctor and helping people in need. Adjoa, the middle daughter, was a talented artist. She yearned for artistic exposure and wanted to explore new mediums and techniques. Kofi, the youngest son, was a gifted athlete. He aimed to compete on a global sports stage and make a name for himself.

Their dreams were not easy to achieve, but the family was determined to make them a reality. The decision to migrate was not an easy one, but they knew that it was the right one for their family.

3

Odyssey Unfolds

The family was on a journey that would take them across Brazil's vast landscapes and Central America's dense forests. This journey was not easy, and they knew that from the start. They were fleeing from their home country, where they had faced persecution and had to leave behind everything they knew and loved. The family's unity and determination were the only things that kept them going through each grueling phase of the journey.

As the family navigated through covert routes, they faced the specter of traffickers and the looming fear of detection. They knew that they could be caught at any moment, which added to the already high level of stress and anxiety they were experiencing. Every day was a new challenge. They had to adapt to their surroundings and rely on their instincts to survive. Every decision they made could have dire consequences, so they had to be extremely careful.

Nights were spent huddled beneath makeshift canopies, with weariness etched onto their faces. The constant fear and uncertainty had taken a toll on them, both physically and emotionally. They had to endure the elements and the discomfort of sleeping on the ground. Despite all the difficulties, they did not give up. Their determination to reach a safer place kept them going.

Each step carried the weight of uncertainty, their resolve strained against the danger of detection and the emotional toll of displacement. They were constantly on the move, never staying in one place for too long. They had to keep a low profile and avoid drawing any attention to themselves. This meant that they had to travel at odd hours and take paths that were less traveled. The family's unity and determination acted as their compass through the labyrinth of challenges they faced. They supported each other through all the difficulties and hardships. They knew that they had to stick together if they were to make it through this journey.

They also had to rely on the kindness of strangers along the way, who helped them when they were in need. As the family journeyed through Central America's dense forests, they encountered new challenges. They had to deal with dangerous animals, rough terrain, and unpredictable weather. They had to adapt quickly to their surroundings and be prepared for anything that came their way. However, they never lost sight of their goal, which was to reach a safer place where they could start a new life.

In conclusion, the family's journey was a difficult one, filled with danger, uncertainty, and hardship. However, their unity and determination helped them through each grueling phase of the journey. They were able to overcome all the challenges they faced, and finally reached a safer place where they could start a new life. Their journey is a testament to the resilience of the human spirit, and a reminder that anything is possible when we are determined and united.

4

Stepping onto Unfamiliar Soil

Cultural duanty, a pulsrly vicsra-thg klwma, ihs, tuchng thsiere ntas ndmutions Kcha, Adijo, and the Acfoan enirrmace ats tnos hamuraticw Mapritatcrso this, atthuns roy this culhtar cat humrrul amcpuifing facace the hem American anrirttider to cuacans to secury shory cansin;d thhoi; the srepulyned the. Amenicant plews thdher halioge stipo in taturrire Adapation to considebile.

The genesis of a new challenge for Kwame, Adjoa, and Kofi began when they set foot on American soil. The land was divergent from their customs and language, and securing shelter and employment proved to be elusive.

Their initial phase in the USA became a complex dance of assimilation and adaptation. It required a delicate balance between preserving their Ghanaian identity and embracing the customs of their adopted homeland. As a family, they grappled with adapting to a novel educational system and societal norms while seeking solace in their shared heritage amidst cultural dissonance.

The family's resilience was palpable as they navigated the maze of unfamiliarity. They tried to find stability in an environment starkly different from their own. The challenges they faced were daunting, but they remained steadfast and determined to succeed in their new home.

For Kwame, Adjoa, and Kofi, the task of adapting to a new culture was not an easy one. They were confronted with a myriad of challenges that tested their patience and perseverance. However, they were determined to succeed and carve out a new life in America.

One of the biggest challenges they faced was finding housing and employment. The cultural differences made it difficult for them to navigate the housing market and secure a suitable place to live. Similarly, finding employment was also a daunting task as their qualifications were not immediately recognized in the US job market.

The family also had to adapt to a new education system, which was vastly different from what they were used to in Ghana. They had to adjust to a new curriculum and teaching style, and this proved to be a significant challenge for them.

Despite the challenges, the family remained resilient. They drew strength from their shared heritage and relied on each other for support.

They found comfort in their cultural traditions and used them as a way to navigate the unfamiliar terrain.

In conclusion, Kwame, Adjoa, and Kofi's journey to America was fraught with challenges. However, their resilience and determination to succeed helped them overcome the obstacles they faced. They proved that with hard work and perseverance, one can adapt to new environments and thrive in unfamiliar territories.

5

Unbroken Bonds

Amidst adversity, the family's bond remained unbroken. Samuel and Abena's unwavering support, the siblings' mutual encouragement, and their shared nostalgia for Ghanaian heritage anchored them in the tumultuous storm of assimilation. The resilience they displayed stemmed not only from their individual aspirations but also from the unwavering support they lent to one another. Each member leaned on the collective strength of the family, drawing from shared experiences and memories of their homeland to weather the challenges of their new life in the USA.

Samuel and Abena, the parents, were pillars of support for their children. They provided a stable home environment while navigating their own challenges as immigrants. Despite their own struggles, they made sure their children had access to opportunities for education and personal growth. They instilled in their children the importance of hard work and community, values deeply ingrained in their Ghanaian culture. These values not only helped the children navigate their new environment but also strengthened the family's bond.

The siblings, too, were instrumental in supporting each other. They shared a common experience of being immigrants in a new culture, and they drew from this shared experience to support each other. They encouraged each other to pursue their goals and dreams, providing emotional support when needed. Even when they faced challenges in their own lives, they always made time to support each other. This mutual encouragement helped them weather even the toughest of storms.

Despite facing adversity, the family held onto their Ghanaian heritage. They celebrated their culture through food, music, and dance, and made sure their children learned about their roots. This helped the children stay connected to their homeland, even as they adjusted to their new life in the USA. The family's heritage also provided a source of strength and resilience, reminding them of their shared history and the obstacles their ancestors had overcome.

In conclusion, the family's bond remained unbroken despite the challenges they faced as immigrants. Samuel and Abena's unwavering support, the siblings' mutual encouragement, and their shared nostalgia for Ghanaian heritage anchored them in the tumultuous storm of assimilation. They drew on their shared experiences and memories of their homeland to weather the challenges of their new life in the USA. Their resilience and strength as a family serve as an inspiration to others facing similar challenges, showing that with mutual support and a strong bond, anything is possible. I hope this helps. Let me know if you need anything else.

6

∾

Navigating Cultural Chasms

As the Ofori family settled into their new life in the USA, they faced a complex challenge of adapting to a new culture while preserving their Ghanaian identity. Kwame, Adjoa, and Kofi found themselves navigating the chasms between the traditions of their homeland and the customs of America. They were determined to find a balance that would allow them to embrace their new life without losing their sense of self.

The family meals were one of the few things that remained a constant in their lives. These meals were steeped in the rich flavors of Ghanaian cuisine and offered a cherished sanctuary, preserving a slice of their home-land amidst the bustling American lifestyle. The family would gather around the table, sharing stories of their day and enjoying the comfort of familiar foods. The aroma of spices, the texture of cassava, and the taste of jollof rice were a reminder of where they came from and what they stood for.

Despite their efforts to preserve their culture, the Ofori family faced challenges in adapting to the American way of life. The educational system in the USA was different from what they were used to in Ghana. The children had to adjust to new norms, such as the emphasis on individualism instead of collectivism. They had to learn new ways of communicating, dress codes, and social etiquette.

The parents, too, found it challenging to navigate the American job market. They had to learn new skills, adapt to different work cultures and find a way to make ends meet. The stress of adjusting to a new way of life took a toll on the family, but they remained committed to their goal of assimilating into American society while preserving their cultural identity.

As time passed, the Ofori family found a way to bridge the gap be-tween their Ghanaian heritage and American culture. They learned to embrace the new while holding on to the old. They found a balance that allowed them to preserve their identity while taking advantage of what America had to offer.

The family's resilience and unity were put to the test in the face of these challenges. But through it all, they remained steadfast in their determination to succeed. They were determined to overcome the obstacles and make a new life for themselves in America.

In conclusion, the Ofori family's story is a testament to the resilience and adaptability of the human spirit. They faced challenges that would have broken many others, but they persevered. By embracing their cultural heritage while adapting to a new way of life, they found a balance that allowed them to thrive. Their story offers hope and inspiration to all who face the challenges of adapting to a new culture while preserving their identity.

7

∽

Community as Sanctuary

It was a difficult time for the family, as they navigated through a labyrinth of trials and tribulations. Each member was forced to face their own set of challenges, but through it all, their bonds grew stronger. They knew that they could rely on each other for support, whether it was financial or emotional.

Kwame was the academic star of the family. Despite the difficulties they faced, he never let his studies falter. He worked hard and sought out scholarships and opportunities to ease the family's financial burden. His dedication and hard work paid off, and he was able to secure a place at one of the top universities in the country.

Adjoa was the family's creative force. She shared her artistic talents with the community, building connections and enriching the family's social circle. Her work was well-known and respected, and she was often asked to contribute to local exhibits and events. Through her art, she was able to bring joy and beauty into the lives of those around her.

Kofi, the youngest member of the family, struggled at first to find his place. But he was determined to contribute in his own way. He found solace and purpose in local sports programs, and soon became an integral part of the community. His enthusiasm and energy were infectious, and he brought a glimmer of hope to the family during a difficult time.

Despite the challenges they faced, the family never gave up. They knew that they had each other, and that together, they could overcome anything. They were a shining example of resilience and perseverance, and their story inspired many others who were going through difficult times.

As time went on, the family continued to grow and thrive. Kwame graduated from university with honors, and went on to start his own successful business. Adjoa's art continued to flourish, and she became a respected teacher and mentor in the community. Kofi went on to become a successful athlete, and was able to use his platform to inspire others to reach for their dreams.

Looking back, the family knew that they had been through a lot. But they also knew that they had come out the other side stronger and more resilient than ever before. They were grateful for each other, and for the love and support that had carried them through some of the toughest times of their lives.

Hurdles of Legalities

The sun had set, and the Ofori family sat in their living room, with a mixture of despair and hopelessness on their faces. Samuel and Abena had come to the United States with their three children, believing that the new land would provide them with a better future. Unfortunately, the legal process had been more complicated than they had anticipated, casting a long shadow over their aspirations.

Samuel and Abena had spent countless hours researching immigration laws, trying to make sense of the complicated legal process. They had hired a lawyer, but the fees had drained their savings. They had applied for various visas, but their applications had been denied multiple times. They had been left with no choice but to live in a state of uncertainty, never knowing what their legal status would be.

The tension in the family had grown over time. The children had felt the financial strain, as their parents struggled to find employment opportunities due to their legal status. The family's unity had been tested, and the stress had taken a toll on their well-being.

Despite the hurdles, the Ofori family clung to the hope that their perseverance would eventually pave a path to stability and security in their new homeland. They kept their heads up, never losing sight of their dreams.

As the days turned into weeks and the weeks into months, Samuel and Abena continued to search for a solution to their legal woes. They attended community meetings, seeking advice and support from other families in similar situations. They spent countless hours on the phone, calling lawyers, and government officials, trying to find a way out of their predicament.

The family's determination paid off when they found a nonprofit organization that provided legal assistance to immigrants. The organization helped them apply for a special visa, and after several months of waiting, they were finally granted the visa.

The sense of relief was palpable in the Ofori household. They had finally received some stability and security in their lives, and the family's unity had been restored. The children could finally focus on their studies, and Samuel and Abena could look for better job opportunities without the fear of being deported.

In conclusion, the Ofori family's journey to stability and security in their new homeland was a challenging one, but their perseverance and hope never wavered. They faced the uncertainty of their legal status with determination, and eventually, they found a solution that worked for them. Their story is a testament to the resilience of the human spirit and the power of hope in the face of adversity

9

Bonds of Resilience

As the family faced numerous trials, their bonds grew stronger. Each member contributed to the family's well-being, whether it was through emotional support or financial contributions within their means.

Despite facing several challenges, Kwame excelled academically and sought scholarships and opportunities to ease the family's financial burdens. Adjoa used her artistic talents to connect with the community, fostering relationships and enriching the family's social fabric. Kofi, who initially faced setbacks, found solace and purpose in local sports programs, adding a ray of hope to the family's journey. Kwame's academic achievements were a source of pride for the entire family.

Despite facing financial difficulties, he remained determined to succeed. He applied for numerous scholarships and was eventually awarded several that helped ease the family's financial burden. Kwame's dedication to his studies was an inspiration to his siblings and parents, who saw firsthand the benefits of hard work and perseverance.

Adjoa, on the other hand, used her artistic talents to connect with the community. She volunteered at local events, showcasing her skills and building relationships with other artists and community members. Adjoa's efforts helped foster a sense of community and belonging, which was especially important for the family during their difficult times. Her positive attitude and willingness to help others inspired her siblings and parents to do the same.

Kofi's love for sports was a silver lining during the family's hardships. Initially, he faced setbacks and struggled to find his place in the community. However, he eventually found solace and purpose in local sports programs. Kofi's involvement in sports helped him improve his physical health, build friendships, and develop a sense of belonging. His enthusiasm for sports was contagious, and soon other family members became involved in sports programs as well.

Through their individual efforts, Kwame, Adjoa, and Kofi strengthened the family's bonds and contributed to their overall well-being. Each member played a unique role in the family's journey, and their combined efforts helped them navigate the labyrinth of trials they faced. Despite the challenges, the family remained united and determined to overcome their difficulties. Their story is a testament to the power of perseverance, hard work, and the strength of family bonds.

10

The Tapestry of Triumph

The sun was setting on the small village in Ghana, casting a warm orange glow over the thatched huts and dusty roads. In one of those huts, the Ofori family was gathered around a small fire, sharing stories and laughter as they savored the simple pleasures of life. But beneath their smiles, there was a sense of unease. The family had been struggling for years to make ends meet, and with each passing day, it seemed like their situation was getting worse.

Despite the challenges they faced, the Ofori family never lost hope. They were a tight-knit group, bound by love and a shared determination to overcome their circumstances. And when an opportunity arose to start a new life in America, they seized it with both hands.

The journey was long and arduous, but the family's spirits never wavered. They arrived in the United States with nothing but hope and a few suitcases, ready to start their new life. The first few months were tough. They struggled to find work and a place to live, but they refused to give up.

Slowly but surely, things started to turn around. The family members found jobs and started to make friends. They immersed themselves in the local culture, blending their Ghanaian heritage with the rhythms of their new American home. And as they settled into their new life, they began to realize that they had something special – something that transcended their individual struggles.

The Ofori family's story echoed resilience, unity, and the triumph of familial ties amidst tribulation. Their journey was not easy, but it was marked by a sense of hope and determination that kept them moving forward, even in the darkest of times. Each member's journey was intertwined yet distinct, painting a picture of fortitude and hope in the pursuit of a better life. And in the blend of their Ghanaian heritage with the rhythms of their new American home, the Ofori family etched a tapestry of triumph – a testament to resilience, unity, and the pursuit of a brighter future.

Today, the Ofori family is thriving. They have a comfortable home, good jobs, and a community that supports them. But they never forget where they came from or the struggles they faced along the way. Their story is a reminder that no matter how hard things get, there is always hope – as long as you have the love and support of those around you.